Karl Johann Philipp Spitta, Richard Massie

Lyra domestica

Christian songs for domestic edification

Karl Johann Philipp Spitta, Richard Massie

Lyra domestica
Christian songs for domestic edification

ISBN/EAN: 9783742843500

Manufactured in Europe, USA, Canada, Australia, Japa

Cover: Foto ©Angelika Wolter / pixelio.de

Manufactured and distributed by brebook publishing software (www.brebook.com)

Karl Johann Philipp Spitta, Richard Massie

Lyra domestica

Lyra Domestica:

CHRISTIAN SONGS for DOMESTIC EDIFICATION.

Translated from the

"Psaltery and Harp" of C. J. P. Spitta

By Richard Massie.

LONDON:
LONGMAN, GREEN, LONGMAN, AND ROBERTS.
1860.

Lyra Domestica:

CHRISTIAN SONGS FOR DOMESTIC EDIFICATION.

Translated from the

"Psaltery and Harp" of C. J. P. Spitta

By Richard Massie.

LONDON:
LONGMAN, GREEN, LONGMAN, AND ROBERTS.
1860.

TO

HIS GRACE THE ARCHBISHOP OF CANTERBURY

THESE HYMNS ARE INSCRIBED

WITH THE DEEPEST FEELINGS OF RESPECT AND VENERATION,

AND WITH A GRATEFUL RECOLLECTION OF

HIS GRACE'S CONNECTION WITH THE DIOCESE OF CHESTER,

BY HIS GRACE'S FAITHFUL AND DEVOTED SERVANT,

THE TRANSLATOR.

PREFACE.

I REMEMBER to have been much ſtruck, ſome years ago, with a remark of James Montgomery, in the preface to the *Chriſtian Pſalmiſt*: "If he who pens theſe ſentiments," ſays that truly Chriſtian poet, "knows his own heart, though it has deceived him too often to be truſted without jealouſy, he would rather be the anonymous author of a few hymns, which ſhould thus become an imperiſhable inheritance to the people of God, than bequeath another epic poem to the world, which ſhould rank his name with Homer, Virgil, and our greater Milton."

It might ſeem preſumptuous in a mere tranſlator to appropriate to himſelf the ſentiments of this original and highly gifted author, to whom we are indebted for ſome of the moſt beautiful hymns in the English language, but I can nevertheless say with truth, that by a somewhat similar feeling I was first induced to undertake the translation which I now offer to the Public. No doubt brighter gems might have been found amid the almost exhaustless mines of German hymnology; no doubt hymns of greater power and beauty might have been selected from the writings of some of the earlier German hymnologists, and especially from those of that sweet singer of Lutheran Germany, Paul Gerhardt; but yet I think it may be doubted, whether any of them would have been so suited to the modern tone of thought as those of Spitta, and so well calculated to promote the object for which they were avowedly written—the edification of the domestic circle. Indeed Miss Winkworth has already culled the choicest flowers from the earlier writers, and transplanted them with so much skill and success into our English soil, that it would be but a discouraging task to follow in her track.

Small as is this collection, it embraces a great variety of subjects, and a cursory glance at the Index will at once show how many important phases of Christian experience are delineated. To quote the words of a friendly critic: "There is hardly a branch of Christian

Preface.

doctrine and morality which they do not touch upon, and on every point they come direct to the reason, feelings, and imagination."

'The versification is remarkably smooth and rhythmical, and the meaning clear and perspicuous. But what particularly distinguishes these hymns is the genuine piety and truly Christian and Catholic feeling which pervades them. Love of Christ and His word is the golden thread which runs through the whole. Is it too much to hope, that, by the Divine blessing, some spark at least of the heavenly feeling which animated the author may be imparted, through the means of this translation, to the heart of the English reader? My labour will not then have been in vain,—if that indeed can be called a labour, which has been the delightful recreation and sweetest solace of my leisure hours.

Addison remarks, in one of the papers of the *Spectator*, that " a reader seldom peruses a book with pleasure till he knows whether the writer of it be a black or a fair man, of a mild or choleric disposition, married, or a bachelor, with other particulars of a like nature that conduce very much to the right understanding of an author." There is much truth in this remark, and I should have been glad if it had been in my power to gratify this natural curiofity by communicating any interesting anecdotes or information respecting the author. All, however, I have yet been able to learn, has been derived from a notice in the *Conversations-Lexicon*, and consists chiefly of a meagre sketch of the leading incidents in Spitta's life, which will, however, prove scarcely more interesting to the English reader than the fireside adventures of the *Vicar of Wakefield*, or his migrations from the blue room to the brown. There is, however, a portrait at the beginning of the book, engraved from a photograph, which will convey to the reader some idea of the author's external lineaments, while those of his heart and mind are with equal fidelity impressed on the hymns themselves.

Carl Johann Philipp Spitta was born at Hanover, on the 1st of August, 1801. After having studied theology at the University of Göttingen from 1821 to 1824, and subsequently been tutor in a private family for some years, he commenced his ministerial labours in the Lutheran Church in the year 1828, as assistant to the pastor of Südwald, in the Grafschaft of Hoya. In 1830 he was appointed chaplain to the garrison and reformatory of Hameln, and I infer from the date, that it was while occupying this post that he published the collection of hymns under the title of *Psalter und*

Harfe, Leipzic, 1833, which has obtained for him a reputation and popularity in Germany only second to that of Paul Gerhardt.

In 1837 he was appointed Pastor at Weshold, in Hoya. In 1847 he was preferred to the high ecclesiastical office of Superintendent, at Wittengen, in the principality of Lüneburg; and in 1853 to that of Superintendent and chief Pastor at Peine, in the principality of Hildersheim. In all these positions he is said to have performed the duties of his sacred office with much zeal, industry, and success.

To this mere outline of facts and dates, I regret to add that of his death, which occurred about the beginning of October, 1859, he being at the time Pastor Primarius and Superintendent, at Burgdorf, in the kingdom of Hanover.

Most of the hymns have been set to music, and a few adapted to congregational singing. I am told that the author frequently sang them himself with his daughters, and so sweet was the harmony of the songs, accompanied by their united voices, that crowds used to assemble under their windows to listen to them.

It may be necessary to apprise the reader, who wishes to compare the translation with the original, that I have ventured to alter the author's arrangement of the hymns, partly because the nature of the subjects seemed to suggest it, but chiefly to procure greater variety in the metre. The repetition of the same form of trochaic measure, occurring as it does in one hymn after another, at the beginning of the book, would have been wearisome to the English ear, particularly as the metre itself is less in unison with the structure and genius of our language than of the German. To obviate any inconvenience which might arise from this change of arrangement, the pages of the English and corresponding German hymn are given in the Index.

I may conclude these remarks with the words of Luther, in his preface to the fine old hymns which he has bequeathed as an invaluable birthright to the German nation:

" Therefore, that such beautiful ornament of music, properly used, may tend to the glory of our blessed Creator, and the edifying of Christians, that He be praised and honoured, and that we, having His holy word impressed on the heart by sweet songs, be strengthened in the faith, may God the Father, Son, and Holy Ghost mercifully grant. Amen." *

R. M.

Pulford, April 1, 1860.

* *Martin Luther's Spiritual Songs*, translated by R. Massie: Hatchard and Son, London; H. Roberts, Chester.

INDEX.

The page in the left-hand column is that of the correſponding hymn in the German.*

Page		Page
1	Up pſaltery and harp	3
94	Morning	6
96	Evening	8
98	Evening devotion	10
86	Joy in creation	11
88	The beauty of nature	13
90	Conſider the lilies of the field	14
92	Winter	16
4	The appearance of Chriſt	18
125	Patience	20
6	Weep not for Me but weep for yourſelves	22
8	Eaſter	24
12	Whit Sunday	27
15	The ſpirit of the Fathers	30
23	The ſong of ſongs	33
35	Comfort in Jeſus' love	34
37	Reſt in God	36

* *Pſalter und Harfe.* Eine Sammlung Chriſtlicher Lieder, zur häuſlichen Erbauung, von Carl Johann Philipp Spitta, 22ſte Auflage. Leipzig, 1854.

Page		Page
40	Self-knowledge	38
43	The Saviour of sinners	40
47	The Lord is my shepherd	44
50	The hour of the Lord	47
52	I am Thine	49
19	See what love!	50
54	My soul is still in God	51
57	Confidence	53
59	I believe	55
64	God's commandments are not hard	57
61	I will abide with Thee	59
66	Ye shall rejoice with unspeakable joy	61
69	Heavenly guidance	64
72	Life and contentment in Jesus	66
29	Turn again	69
75	The vanity of the world	71
78	Our conversation is in heaven	73
81	The servant of the Lord	76
84	Strong in faith, rich in love	79
100	Salvation is come to this house	81
21	The word of life	83
102	The life of faith	85
27	Unity in the Spirit	87
104	The Blessing of Christian fellowship	89
99	Comfort in the night	91
107	Devotion	92
108	Work in the Lord	93
24	The Missionaries	95
110	The Father loveth you	97
113	Faithful in little things	100
116	I and my house will serve the Lord	103
119	The happy lot	106
122	Abide in Jesus	108
124	The Christian's cross	110
127	Be ready for the days are evil	111

Index.

Page		Page
129	Longing	113
32	My soul thirsteth after the living God	115
132	Encouragement	117
135	The plant of God's planting	119
137	A time of dearth	121
140	Father, Son, and Holy Ghost	124
142	Comfort	126
145	Pilgrim's song	128
149	Parting	130
147	Home-sickness	132
151	The Song of dying	134
153	Christ has taken away the power of death	136
155	The grave	138
157	What we shall be	140

LYRA DOMESTICA.

B

Lyra Domestica.

UP! PSALTERY AND HARP.

LONELY was the way and dreary
    Once to Canaan's fair abode;
Few there were, who, faint and weary,
    Trod the unfrequented road:
For by thousands mocked and chidden,
    They pursued the dangerous way,
Which appeared as though forbidden
    And beneath a curse it lay.

True it is, that Sion's daughters
    Never their sweet home forgat;
By Euphrates' silent waters
    Weeping and deprest they sat:
On the willow-trees beside them
    Hung their harps; for none would sing,
In a land where foes deride them,
    Songs of praise to Sion's King.

As they spake to one another
  Of the Lord's beloved abode,
Sighs burst forth they could not smother,
  Tears of bitter anguish flowed :
For the Heathen hordes had wasted
  God's own house with open shame,
Till the Lord from Heaven hasted
  To the help of His great name.

From the neighbouring hills descending,
  Heralds peaceful tidings bear;
Songs of home and joy are rending
  With sweet sounds the startled air.
On they press o'er hill and valley,
  E'en the desert teems with life,
And should any seem to dally,
  They are urged with friendly strife.

Yes! the Lord Himself hath spoken;
  Strike your tents, be glad of heart;
He whose word can not be broken,
  Saith, "from Babylon depart."
God hath heard your sighs, and ended
  Many a year of grief and wrong;
Take your harps so long suspended,
  Join ye all in grateful song.

God, renowned in Israel's story,
  My Redeemer, God, and King,
I will magnify Thy glory
  With sweet psalms and tuneful string.

Grateful tribute ever bringing,
　　I will praife Thee night and day,
Songs of joy and triumph finging,
　　As I climb the narrow way.

MORNING.

THE purple morning gilds the Eastern
skies,
And what the night had hidden from
our eyes
Now stands revealed to our ad-
miring gaze;
Mountain and valley, wood and fruitful plain,
Which in their misty bed asleep had lain,
Shine forth and glitter in the sun's bright rays.

Shine in my soul, and light and joy impart,
O blessed Jesus, Sun of my dark heart,
O cause therein the light of truth to shine;
Show me each crooked winding of my heart,
Change and renew it so in every part,
That my whole nature be transformed to Thine.

Lord, in Thy light O let me walk this day,
By Thy love prompted, act, and speak, and pray,
As a new creature it becomes to do,
Whose aim it is, in all his words and ways,
To set forth duly his Creator's praise,
And new in heart, in life be also new.

I pray not, " take my troubles all away; "
It is for love to bear them that I pray,

And firm belief that all is for my good;
That every trouble must be kindly meant,
Since from the hands of Him it has been sent,
  Who is my loving Father and my God.

I pray not that my days may smoothly run;
Ah no! I pray, Thy will alone be done!
  Yet give a childlike trusting heart to me;
Should the earth seek to draw my spirit down,
O let my heart continue still Thine own,
  And draw me upward from the earth to Thee.

I pray not, Lord, that Thou wilt quickly end
The griefs and troubles Thou art pleased to send;
  Be Thou my peace in every trying hour.
I ask not Heaven at once to enter in,
But ere I die, that I may die to sin,
  Be Thou its death: destroy its guilt and power.

Thou Sun, by whom my new life first was lighted,
O let me not again become benighted,
  But be my light when shades around me spread;
With the bright splendour of Thy heavenly rays
Illuminate the evening of my days,
  And shed a halo round my dying head.

EVENING.

O LORD, who by Thy prefence haft made light
    The heat and burden of the toilfome day,
Be with me alfo in the filent night,
    Be with me when the daylight fades away.
As Thou haft given me ftrength upon the way,
    So deign at evening to become my gueft,
As Thou haft fhared the labours of the day,
    So alfo deign to fhare and blefs my reft.

No ftep difturbs me, not a found is heard,
    I commune in my chamber and am ftill,
And mufe with deep attention on Thy word,
    The faithful record of Thy mind and will.
O fpeak a word of bleffing, gracious Lord,
    Thy bleffing is endued with foothing power;
On the poor heart worn out with toil Thy word
    Falls foft and gentle as the evening fhower.

How fad and cold, if Thou be abfent, Lord,
    The evening leaves me, and my heart how dead!
But if Thy prefence grace my humble board,
    I feem with heavenly manna to be fed;

Fraught with rich blessing, breathing sweet repose,
  The calm of evening settles on my breast;
If Thou be with me when my labours close,
  No more is needed to complete my rest.

Come then, O Lord, and deign to be my guest
  After the day's confusion, toil, and din,
O come to bring me peace, and joy, and rest,
  To give salvation and to pardon sin.
Bind up the wounds, assuage the aching smart
  Left in my bosom from the day just past,
And let me on a Father's loving heart
  Forget my griefs and find sweet rest at last.

EVENING DEVOTION.

OW smiling the day departed,
   How sweetly evening steals on!
How jocund and how merry-hearted
   The birds sing their evening song!

The flowers have no power of saying
   Their prayers with audible sound,
And yet are they silently praying,
   As they bend their heads to the ground.

Wherever I look is devotion,
   God's praise is the general theme,
From the distant boom of the ocean
   To the voice of the murmuring stream.

And all around us is praying
   For rest from the toils of the day,
And seems as though it were saying,
   Poor mortal, do thou also pray!

JOY IN CREATION.

O THOU beautiful Creation,
    Which the Lord's creative hand
For our joy and admiration
    Hath so wonderfully planned!
O how varied are thy features,
    O what love is there difplayed,
To delight and blefs the creatures,
    Which His power and wifdom made!

In the high and heavenly places,
    In the loweft e'er explored,
We difcern the plaineft traces
    Of the goodnefs of the Lord!
Earth and air, and boundlefs ocean,
    All are mirrors, where we fee,
Now in ftillnefs, now in motion,
    Love in its immenfity.

At a diftance, and in nearnefs,
    In the ftar, and in the flower,
Are infcribed with truth and clearnefs
    God's great wifdom, love, and power.
Every where we fee the traces,
    Which a child may underftand,
Of a God, whofe love embraces
    All the works of His own hand.

Oh! how sweet it is from Nature
    To look up to Nature's God!
To a merciful Creator,
    Who in all things seeks our good;
Who deserves the consecration
    Of all powers which we possess,
Worship, praise and adoration,
    More than tongue can e'er express.

Yes! I know thee, revelation
    Of my Lord in Nature traced,
Since not only in Creation
    I have learnt to see and taste
Thy great love, and mark its traces,
    But in Jesus Christ have found
Love, which every love surpasses,
    Grace, no mortal man can found.

THE BEAUTY OF NATURE.

REJOICE in the beautiful earth,
    For well she deserveth our praise,
What tongue can declare all the worth,
    Which God to adorn her displays!

And yet tho' so richly endowed,
    She is only the work of His hands,
A creature, which well may be proud
    To do whatsoe'er He commands.

Rejoice in the moon and the sun,
    And the stars brightly shining by night,
As the course, God appoints them, they run,
    And lend us their lustre and light.

And yet, while they shine on our globe,
    They are only the work of His hands,
The spangles adorning His robe,
    The creatures that wait His command.

If then but His handiwork here
    Such blessings already impart,
O what must our rapture be there,
    To repose on His fatherly heart!

CONSIDER THE LILIES OF THE FIELD!

SWEET lily of the field, declare
   Whofe hand it was that made,
And in fuch beauty placed thee there,
   Before mine eyes difplayed?

How white the robe which thou haft on,
   With golden duft o'erlaid!
In all his glory, Solomon
   Like thee was not arrayed.

God raifed thee from the earth, fweet flower,
   And tends thee with delight,
And fends thee, in the ftill calm hour,
   An angel in the night.

Thy robes he wafhes in the dew,
   And dries them in the air,
And bleaches them in funfhine too,
   To make them bright and fair.

Sweet lily of the field, although
   Thou haft no voice nor fpeech,
Thou doft a bright example fhow,
   A ufeful leffon teach.

Sweet lily of the field, by thee
    This lesson I am taught:
"God cares for little flowers like me,
    Take then no anxious thought."

WINTER.

T is winter. All ſeems dead or dying,
    Solitude throughout all nature reigns;
She herſelf, like ſome fair corpſe, is lying
    In the ſheet, which ſhrouds her wide domains.
Her dear children ſleep beneath their awning,
    Sheltered ſafely in their mother's breaſt,
Dreaming of the reſurrection morning,
    When the ſpring ſhall wake them from their reſt.

Thou O earth, art ſtript of all thy beauty,
    All thy boaſted glory now has fled,
Thou thyſelf doſt preach to us our duty
    In a ſolemn ſermon o'er the dead.
Earth can yield us no enduring pleaſure,
    We muſt part from that which moſt we love;
Would'ſt thou ſeek an everlaſting treaſure,
    Raiſe thy thoughts to heaven and things above.

Let the earth herſelf to heaven direct thee,
    Seek not here thy home, but journey on
To the manſions, where the friends expect thee,
    Who before thee are already gone.
Vainly ſeek'ſt thou here what thou deſireſt,
    Therefore ſpeed thee on thy heavenward way;
Every thing which thou from earth requireſt,
    Is enough to hide thy mouldering clay.

But when Easter songs again awaken
    Those, who still are sleeping in the dust,
Earth shall bring the treasures she has taken,
    And discharge her solemn sacred trust.
Think not here to find enduring pleasure,
    Earth possesses nothing of her own;
Let her lead thee to the one true treasure,
    Joy in heaven at God's eternal throne.

THE APPEARANCE OF CHRIST.

CHRIST, whose first appearance lighted
   Gloomy death's obscure domain,
Long in Herod's courts benighted
   Sought I Thee, but sought in vain:
All was glitter, pomp, and pleasure,
   Sensuality, and pride;
But my heart found not its treasure,
   And remained unsatisfied.

Then to learned scribes and sages
   Seeking Christ I wandered on,
But upon their barren pages
   Jacob's star had never shone:
True indeed, like men in prison
   Groping for the light of day,
Spake they of the light new-risen,
   But themselves saw not one ray.

To the temple I was guided
   By the altar-fire and lights,
But though all else was provided,
   Christ was absent from the rites.
Then more precious time I wasted
   In thy streets, Jerusalem,
But I sought in vain, and hasted
   On my way to Bethlehem.

In the streets I wandered slowly,
    Looking for some trusty guide;
All was dark and melancholy,
    None I met with far and wide.
On a sudden I perceivèd
    O'er my head a star to shine;
Lo! because I had believèd,
    And had sought Him, Christ was mine.

Only seek, and you will find Him,
    Never cease to seek the Lord;
And should He delay, remind Him
    Boldly of His plighted word.
Follow Him, and He will lead you;
    Trust Him in the darkest night;
Jacob's star will still precede you,
    Jacob's star will give you light.

PATIENCE.

A GENTLE angel wendeth
  Throughout this world of woe,
Whom God in mercy sendeth
  To comfort us below.
Her looks a peace abiding
  And holy love proclaim;
O follow then her guiding,
  Sweet Patience is her name!

She leads us through this tearful
  And sorrow-stricken land,
And speaks, resigned and cheerful,
  Of better days at hand:
And when thou art despairing,
  She bids thee clear thy brow,
Herself thy burden sharing,
  More hopeful far than thou.

She sobers into sadness
  Thy grief's excessive smart,
And steeps in peace the madness
  And tumult of the heart.
The darkest hour she maketh
  As bright as sun at noon,
And heals each wound that acheth,
  Full surely, if not soon.

Thy falling tears she chides not,
   But pours in healing balm;
Thy longing she derides not,
   But makes devout and calm:
And when in stormy seasons
   Thou askest, murmuring, why?
She giveth thee no reasons,
   But smiling points on high.

To every doubt and question
   She cares not to reply;
" Bear on," is her suggestion,
   " Thy resting-place is nigh."
Thus by thy side she walketh,
   A true and constant friend,
Not overmuch she talketh,
   But thinks " O happy end!"

WEEP NOT FOR ME, BUT WEEP FOR YOURSELVES.

WHEREFORE weep we over Jesus,
 O'er His death and bitter smart?
Weep we rather, that He sees us
 Unconvinced and hard of heart:
For His soul was never tainted
 With the smallest spot or stain,
T'was for us He was acquainted
 With such depths of grief and pain.

Oh! what profits it with groaning
 Underneath His cross to stand;
Ah! what profits our bemoaning
 His pale brow and bleeding hand;
Wherefore gaze on Him expiring,
 Railed at, pierced, and crucified,
Whilst we think not of inquiring,
 Wherefore and for whom He died?

If no sin could be discovered
 In the pure and spotless Lord,
If the cruel death He suffered
 Is sin's just and meet reward:
Then it must have been for others
 That the Lord on Calvary bled,
And the guilt have been a brother's,
 Which was laid upon His head.

And for whom hath He contended
  In a strife so strange and new?
And for whom to hell descended?
  Brothers! 'twas for me and you!
Now you see that He was reaping
  Punishment for us alone;
And we have great cause for weeping,
  Not for His guilt, but our own.

If we then make full confession,
  Joined with penitence and prayer,
If we see our own transgression
  In the punishment He bare,
If we mourn with true repentance,
  We shall hear the Saviour say:
"Fear not, I have borne your sentence,
  Wipe your bitter tears away."

EASTER DAY.

SUN, shine forth in all thy splendour,
  Joyfully pursue thy way,
For thy Lord and my Defender
  Rose triumphant on this day.
When He bowed His head, sore troubled
  Thou didst hide thyself in night;
Shine forth now with rays redoubled,
  He is risen who is thy light.

Earth, be joyous and glad-hearted,
  Spread out all thy vernal bloom;
For thy Lord is not departed,
  He has broken through the tomb.
When the Lord expired, wide-yawning
  Thy strong rocks were rent with fright;
Greet thy risen Lord this morning,
  Bathed in floods of rosy light.

Say, my soul, what preparation
  Makest thou for this high day,
When the God of thy salvation
  Opened through the tomb a way?
Dwellest thou with pure affection
  On this proof of power and love?
Doth thy Saviour's resurrection
  Raise thy thoughts to things above?

Haſt thou, borne on Faith's ſtrong pinion,
   Riſen with the riſen Lord ?
And, releaſed from ſin's dominion,
   Into purer regions ſoared ?
Or art thou, in ſpite of warning,
   Dead in trespasses and ſin ?
Hath to thee the purple morning
   No true Eaſter uſhered in ?

O then let not death o'ertake thee
   By the ſhades of night o'erſpread;
See! thy Lord is come to wake thee,
   He is riſen from the dead.
While the time as yet allows thee,
   Hear; the gracious Saviour cries,
"Sleeper, from thy ſloth arouſe thee,
   To new life at once ariſe."

See, with looks of tender pity
   He extends his wounded hands,
Bidding thee, with fond entreaty,
   Shake off ſin's enthralling bands:
"Wait not for ſome future meetneſs,
   Dread no puniſhment from me,
Rouſe thyself and taste the ſweetneſs
   Of the new life offered thee."

Let no precious time be waſted,
   To new life ariſe at length,
He who death for thee hath tasted,
   For new life will give new strength.

Try to rise, at once bestir thee,
   Still press on and persevere,
Let no weariness deter thee,
   He who woke thee still is near.

Waste not so much time in weighing
   When and where thou shalt begin;
Too much thinking is delaying,
   Rivets but the chains of sin.
He will help thee, and provide thee
   With a courage not thine own,
Bear thee in His arms and guide thee,
   Till thou learn'st to walk alone.

See! thy Lord Himself is risen,
   That thou mightest also rise,
And emerge from sin's dark prison
   To new life and open skies.
Come to Him who can unbind thee,
   And reverse thy awful doom,
Come to Him, and leave behind thee
   Thy old life—an empty tomb!

WHITSUNDAY.

DRAW, Holy Spirit, nearer,
    And in our hearts abide;
O make our judgment clearer,
    Our minds inform and guide.
O come, Thou great Renewer,
    Touch heart and lip with fire;
Make every bofom truer,
    Our aims and objects higher.

O come, Thou true Confoler,
    Thou Fire, that warms the cold,
The haughty breaft's Controler,
    O come and make us bold.
On all fides danger threatens;
    Lord, to our fuccour come,
And arm us with the weapons
    Of early Chriftendom.

Hard unbelief and folly
    The truth of God deny;
O arm us, Lord moft holy,
    With weapons from on high,
With faith that never falters,
    Unmoved by fear or praife,
With love that never alters,
    And hope in darkeft days.

We need a free confefsion
   In this our lukewarm age,
A frank and full profefsion
   In spite of fcorn and rage;
To friend alike and foeman,
   On this or heathen ground,
To every man and woman
   The Gofpel trump to found.

Where'er Thy Word is founded,
   In far and favage lands,
The Heathen are confounded,
   And caft off Satan's bands.
On every fide they waken
   To hear Thy blefsed Word:
Shall it from us be taken,
   By us remain unheard?

On us, O Thou most holy,
   Thy wrath doth justly fall,
Who hear, yet, through our folly,
   Have not obeyed the call.
Let us with deep proftration
   Implore God's grace, that thus
The Word of His falvation
   Be not withdrawn from us.

Give power to thofe who witnefs
   And preach Thy holy Word,
That all may tafte its fweetnefs,
   And rally round the Lord.

Be this our preparation,
   A heart and tongue of fire!
That this our proclamation
   May ſpeed as we deſire.

THE SPIRIT OF THE FATHERS.

SPIRIT, by whose operation
    Faith and holiness proceed,
Source of heavenly conversation,
    Strength in weakness, help in need!
Spirit, by whose inspiration
    Prophets and Apostles spake,
Martyrs bled, and tribulation
    Saints endured for Jesus' sake!

Lord, endue us with Thy blessing,
    That, though babes we be in grace,
Faith, and love, and zeal possessing
    For Thy house and holy place;
We may stake our dearest treasures,
    All the good things of this life,
Honour, wealth, and darling pleasures,
    In the great and holy strife.

Give us Abram's faith unshaken,
    That the promise must be true,
And what God hath undertaken,
    He assuredly will do;
Which not only could unmovèd
    Trust the covenant of grace,
But the thing which he most lovèd
    At the Lord's disposal place.

Give us Joseph's chaste behaviour,
   When the world with crafty wiles
Seeks to draw us from the Saviour
   To herself, with frowns or smiles.
Give us grace and strength for shunning
   This ensnaring Potiphar,
Wisdom to elude her cunning,
   Strength her open hate to bear.

Give us Moses' intercession,
   When he pleaded, wept, and prayed,
That the people's sore transgression
   Might not to their charge be laid.
Let us not with selfish coldness
   See the sinner go astray,
But with Moses' holy boldness
   Plead and wrestle, weep and pray.

Give us David's bold defiance
   Of the Lord's and Israel's foes,
And, in trouble, the reliance
   Which on God his rock he shows;
His right princely disposition,
   Friendship, constancy, and truth,
But still more his deep contrition
   For the errors of his youth.

Arm us with the stern decision
   Of Elijah, in these days,
When men, led by superstition,
   To false Gods new altars raise.

Let us shun the mere profession
  Common in our days and land,
Witnessing a good confession,
  Even if alone we stand.

Give us the Apostles' daring,
  And their bold undaunted mood,
Threats and fierce reproaches bearing,
  To proclaim a Saviour's blood.
Let us to the truth bear witness,
  Which alone can make us free,
Nor leave off, until its sweetness
  All shall taste and know through Thee.

Give us Stephen's look collected,
  And his calm and cheerful mind,
When we meet with unexpected
  Trials of the sharpest kind.
In the midst of shouts and crying,
  Let us with composure stand,
Open heaven to us in dying,
  Show us Christ at God's right hand.

Spirit, by whose operation
  Faith and love and might are given,
Source of holy conversation,
  Bearing seed and fruit for heaven;
Spirit, by whose inspiration
  Prophets and Apostles spake,
Visit us with Thy salvation,
  Dwell with us for Jesus' sake.

THE SONG OF SONGS.

THERE is a song so thrilling,
  So far all songs excelling,
That they who sing it, sing it oft again;
  No mortal did invent it,
  But God by Angels sent it,
So deep and earnest, yet so sweet and plain.

  The love, which it revealeth,
  All earthly sorrows healeth;
They flee like mist before the break of day.
  When, O my soul, thou learnest
  That song of songs in earnest,
  Thy cares and troubles all shall pass away.

COMFORT IN JESUS' LOVE.

STILL on Thy loving heart let me repose,
    Jesus, sweet Author of my joy and rest;
    O let me pour my sorrows, cares, and woes,
Into Thy true and sympathising breast.
Thy love grows never cold, but its pure flame
    Seems every day more strong and bright to glow,
Thy truth remains eternally the same,
    Pure and unsullied as the mountain snow.

O what is other love compared with Thine,
    Of such high value, such eternal worth!
What is man's love compared with love divine,
    Which never changes in this changing earth;
Love, which in this cold world grows never cold,
    Love, which decays not with the world's decay,
Love, which is young when all things else grow old,
    Which lives when heaven and earth shall pass away?

How little love unchangeable and fixed
    In this dark valley doth to man remain,
With what unworthy motive is it mixed,
    How full of grief, uncertainty, and pain!

Love is the object, which attracts all eyes,
   We win it, and already fear to part,
A thousand rivals watch to seize the prize
   And tear the precious idol from our heart.

   But Thou, in spite of our offences past,
And those, alas! which still in us are found,
   Hast loved us, Jesus, with a love so vast,
No span can reach it, and no plummet found.
   Though the poor love we give Thee in return
Should be extinguished, Thine is ever true,
Its vestal fire eternally doth burn,
   Though everlasting, always fresh and new.

Thou, who art ever ready to embrace
   All those, who truly after Thee enquire,
Thou, who hast promised in Thy heart a place
   To all who love Thee and a place desire;
O Lord, when I am anxious and deprest,
   And dim with tears mine eyes can hardly see,
O let me lean upon Thy faithful breast,
   Rejoicing that e'en I am loved by Thee.

REST IN GOD.

N vain thou seekest in thyself to find
   Light, life, and joy, or any lasting
     peace;
   Return to God, seek Him with all
     thy mind,
The one true source of life and happiness.
Return to Him, poor erring child of man,
   Where first thy being and thy life began,
Let all thy longings be to Him addrest,
   Then and then only shalt thou find true rest.

But ah! thou can'st not go to Him, for see!
   A mighty wall of separation stands
Built up by sin between thy God and thee:
   Behold! thy Saviour stretches out His hands,
And opens to thee through His precious blood
   A way of peace and access to thy God:
He, who broke down that wall and sets thee free,
   Hath borne thy guilt and thy iniquity.

Lo! thy Creator gave thee life at first,
   Thy Saviour doth a second life bestow;
He gives thee water to assuage thy thirst,
   A guide to lead thee through this vale of woe;

His Spirit giveth sight unto the blind,
  Peace to the heart and clearness to the mind,
New strength and motives virtue to pursue,
  The love of God, and heaven itself in view.

Behold thee now returned to thy true rest!
  Through the thin veil of time thy joyful eyes
Discern the happy mansions of the blest
  And heaven's bright walls in dim perspective rise.
In fear no longer of a Father's rod,
  Thou feel'st that thou art reconciled to God,
And though thy troubles do not wholly cease,
  Hast a sweet foretaste of thy future bliss.

Then seek not here in vain a resting place,
  Nor in thyself expect to find repose;
Such seeking only aggravates thy case,
  And is embittered with a thousand woes;
Such seeking wearies, but can not impart
  The peace it longs for to the aching heart;
Sleep may weigh down the eyes by care opprest,
But heavy slumber is not peaceful rest.

Cradle an infant on the softest bed,
  Soothe it with songs of lullaby to rest;
More gently will it lay its little head,
  More sweetly slumber on its mother's breast;
Where the first draught of health and life it found,
  There will its sleep be sweet, its slumber sound;
Return my soul to God, thine only rest,
  Then and then only art thou truly blest.

SELF-KNOWLEDGE.

MAN hath his anxious seasons,
    Much pain not understood;
Nor can he tell his reasons,
    Till he discovers God:
When first he comprehendeth
    How just He is and true,
His dream of goodness endeth,
    His sins come all to view.

With Thee, O Lord, acquainted,
    He learns to look within,
And sees his heart is tainted,
    And full, alas! of sin.
From Thy great power he learneth
    How vile he is and base,
His nakedness discerneth
    In Thy abounding grace.

O goodness past expression!
    Which brings not to our view
The height of our transgression,
    Until it shews us too
A mode of expiation
    Through Christ's atoning blood,
A full and free salvation,
    And blissful rest with God!

What need we to content us,
   Since God gives us so much?
What fears can now torment us?
   Since His great love was such,
That ere we comprehended
   Our sin, distress, and loss,
The mighty work was ended
   Which saved us on the cross.

Should greater be my gladness
   That Thou such love dost shew,
Or greater still my sadness
   That I have grieved Thee so?
Oh! both alike are needful,
   To know how poor I be,
And yet not be unheedful
   How rich I am in Thee.

O happy hour of sadness
   And pain not understood!
Which endeth in such gladness
   And everlasting good.
Mine eyes upraised to heaven
   With tears of joy run o'er;
I know I am forgiven;
   Ah! what can I want more?

THE SAVIOUR OF SINNERS.

JESUS, Friend of sinners,
  Move my soul, I pray Thee,
  Both to choose Thee and obey Thee,
  And in Thee discover
  Daily some new treasure,
Depths of love no line can measure;
O may I,
Drawn thereby,
Follow, where Thou goest,
Who the true way shewest.

While my life remaineth,
Deepen my impression
Of the guilt and great transgression
Which Thou hast forgiven;
That my heart's affection,
Sweetly drawn by this reflection,
May arise
To the skies,
With Thee ever living,
By faith, with thanksgiving.

Daily I discover
Some new sin or other,
Which if Thou, Lord, didst not cover,
I might justly tremble;

I am weak and ailing,
Daily stumbling, hourly failing:
But Thy blood,
Lamb of God!
Which from all sin cleanses,
Blots out my offences.

Ere the voice of Jesus
Yet had found and called me,
Sin, alas! had so enthralled me,
And so firmly bound me,
That without resistance,
Helpless, hopeless of assistance,
To her sway
Night and day,
I alas! consented,
Though by her tormented.

But since Thou, my Saviour,
Didst bring help and freedom
From this spiritual Edom,
Tho' Sin hath no longer
In vile bondage held me,
Nor to do her will compelled me;
Yet doth she
Constantly
Struggle to recall me,
And again enthrall me.

Ah! Thou com'st to help me
With Thy blessed promise,

That Sin shall not overcome us;
And should'st Thou permit us
Now and then to stumble,
'Tis alone to keep us humble;
Soon would Sin
Victory win,
Didst not Thou defend us,
And Thy succour lend us.

Thou art still our helper,
For us interceding,
With the Father warmly pleading,
That He would forgive us
All our great offences,
And bear with our negligences.
To us all,
When we fall,
Thy blood brings sweet healing,
Our forgiveness sealing.

Through the blood of Jesus
We have now remission
Of our sins, and free admission
Into the most Holy;
Nor will He forsake us
Though sin should sometimes o'ertake us:
They are clean
From all sin,
Who in Him are living,
Sprinkled, washed, forgiven.

Truth by man unfathomed!
Love that hath no ending,

Grace all human thought transcending!
Who can e'er forget it?
How He died to save us!
How He pitied and forgave us!
Who can them
Now condemn,
Whom He hath forgiven,
And made heirs of heaven?

THE LORD IS MY SHEPHERD.

I HEAR my Shepherd calling,
  And inftantly obey,
And climb, though fometimes falling,
  The fteep and rugged way.
Though often at a diftance,
  I ftrive to follow ftill,
And offer no refiftance
  To His moft bleffed will.

Thou fhew'ft Thyfelf the greateft,
  When greateft my diftrefs,
Thy comforts are the fweeteft
  In days of bitternefs.
Sometimes my courage fails me,
  My ftrength feems well nigh gone,
But ftill Thy grace avails me,
  Thy ftrength ftill helps me on.

Sometimes I figh for morning
  In forrow's gloomy night,
When lo ! already dawning
  The day brings joy and light.
Sometimes my griefs enclofe me
  In every form and fhape,
But God in mercy fhews me
  A method of efcape.

Sometimes dark thoughts steal o'er me
    Here in this vale of tears,
The future spread before me
    So overcast appears;
The word of Thy salvation
    Speaks comfort to my breast,
In midst of tribulation
    I find in Thee true rest.

Old sins oft leave behind them
    Deep scars, which wound me still;
Thou knowest how to bind them,
    And heal them with great skill.
I often sink down weary
    And heart-sick on the road,
But Thou art nigh to cheer me
    And ease me of my load.

My gracious Guide and Master,
    Thy wandering sheep O seek,
Fain would I follow faster,
    But am, alas! too weak:
O come to help and guide me,
    When I can not proceed,
If Thou art, Lord, beside me,
    I must perforce succeed.

Soon shall I cease to wander;
    The day may be at hand,
When Thou shalt take me yonder
    To my dear Fatherland;

There shall my chief employment
    Consist in praising Thee,
With ever new enjoyment,
    Throughout eternity.

THE HOUR OF THE LORD.

'TIS not yet the hour appointed!
   I make anfwer to my heart,
When depreft and difappointed
   It is longing to depart:
Wait awhile and hold thee ftill,
He doth well who waits God's will.

When a thoufand griefs and troubles
   Leave no reft by day or night,
When the ftorm its force redoubles,
   And is almoft at its height;
Patiently abide His will
At whofe word the waves are ftill.

Every veffel muft be drainèd,
   Cups of joy and cups of grief,
Truft in God with faith unfeignèd,
   Look to Him for thy relief;
When all human counfel fails,
Then it is that God prevails.

When the flood is rifing higher,
   Till it overflows the brink,
Then the Comforter draws nigher,
   Ah! much nigher than we think,
For it grieves Him to the heart
To behold our bitter fmart.

Ah! it is with no hard Master,
    No hard Lord we have to do,
If we bear each new disaster
    With calm faith and patience too,
We shall soon experience this :
It will come,—that hour of bliss.

Dost thou, heart, demand some token
    That the Lord will give thee rest?
Trust the word which He hath spoken,
    His own time must be the best;
Suffer, trust, and hope on still,
End right well it must and will.

O the hour of our exemption
    From all pain, distress, and woe!
O the hour of our redemption
    E'en from death our last grim foe!
Sweet as sunshine after shower
Will be that all-glorious hour.

I AM THINE.

THY will I cheerfully obey,
Both when Thou giv'st and tak'st away;
I follow, wheresoe'er Thou leadest,
I shun whatever Thou forbiddest;
Do as Thou wilt, O Lord, provided
I never be from Thee divided.

I am not bent on mine own will,
But rather wish, devout and still,
To make Thy blessed will and pleasure
The rule by which mine own I measure;
To Thee alone my ways commending
From the beginning to the ending.

I were indeed a very fool
To make mine own blind will my rule:
I have a thousand times outwitted,
Deceived, betrayed myself, and cheated,
Nor have I ever found a blessing
In ways self-chosen and self-pleasing.

Through all my life how graciously
Hast Thou, my Saviour, dealt with me!
How often kept my feet from falling,
And heard me e'en before my calling!
Nor should I e'er have chosen Thee,
Hadst Thou not, Lord, first chosen me.

SEE WHAT LOVE!

SEE, O see, what love the Father
　　Hath bestowed upon our race,
How He bends with sweet compassion
　　Over us His beaming face!
See how He His best and dearest
　　For the very worst hath given,
His own Son for us poor sinners,
　　See, O see, the love of heaven!

See, O see, what love the Saviour
　　Also hath on us bestowed,
How He bled for us and suffered,
　　How He bare the heavy load!
On the cross and in the garden
　　Oh how sore was His distress!
Is not this a love that passeth
　　Aught that tongue can e'er express?

See, O see, what love is shewn us
　　Also by the Holy Ghost!
How He strives with us poor sinners
　　Even when we sin the most,
Teaching, comforting, correcting,
　　Where He sees it needful is!
O what heart would not be thankful
　　For a three-fold love like this?

MY SOUL IS STILL IN GOD.

MY soul in God abideth still
    And ceaseth her complaining;
Let Him do with me what He will,
    While life is yet remaining:
He is my Lord, His servant I,
Do what He will, I ask not why;
    His ways are truth and mercy.

And yet 'tis hard to be quite still
    And by distrust offend not,
When things appear to turn out ill,
    And God we comprehend not:
Blind Reason summons to her bar
God's Providence for things that are
    Too deep for her to fathom!

"Why this, why that," we oft demand
    In our presumptuous cavil;
"This tangled web the wisest hand
    Can surely not unravel:
Surely my troubles are too great,
I have deserved a better fate
    Than Providence allots me."

Meantime my God is silent long,
    Until the glorious issue

Shews that no thread was woven wrong
    In all the wondrous tissue;
Until at last the hour is come,
When full of shame I must stand dumb
    In presence of my Maker.

Therefore, my soul, abide thou still
    In God, in every season,
Who orders all things by His will
    And not thy feeble reason;
And when the end shall make quite clear
The things which now so dark appear,
    Thou shalt give God the glory.

Then wilt thou have great cause for praise,
    That, conscious of thy blindness,
Thou didst not murmur in dark days,
    Nor doubt God's loving kindness;
And when thy waiting time is o'er,
Thou shalt praise God for evermore
    For all His wondrous mercies.

CONFIDENCE.

I PLACE myself in Jesus' hands
    And there abide for ever;
No griefs, no joys, shall loose the bands,
    Nor our sweet union sever;
In those dread days
When earth decays,
Who stays on Him, and whom He stays,
    Shall be preserved for ever.

A rock and castle is the Lord,
    And they shall see and wonder,
Who build on His almighty word,
    And thereon deeply ponder;
And what He saith,
In life and death,
My heart shall trust with steadfast faith,
    Though earth be rent asunder.

Let Him do with me what He will,
    He cannot fail to please me,
I cleave to Him with strong faith still,
    And hope that He will bless me:
He must be blest
Who loves Him best,
And on His word doth firmly rest;
    Lord, with this truth impress me.

When things are at their worst, I will
    Still joy in His protection,
Who loves to bring out good from ill,
    And grieves in my affliction:
His trials sent
Are all well meant,
His blows a Father's chastisement,
    And tokens of affection.

My confidence unshaken stands
    Upon His blessed promise,
That none shall pluck us from His hands,
    Nor any foe o'ercome us.
He will not break
The word He spake,
He will not leave us nor forsake,
    Nor take His Spirit from us.

I BELIEVE.

BELIEVE, and so have spoken:
    Hear what God hath done for
      me!
I believe, and by this token
    I confess Him openly:
That there is no name, whereby
    Sinners can be saved, but His,
God Himself, the Lord Most High,
    Jesus Christ our Righteousness.

I believe, and therefore ever
    Will I love my God and guide;
I believe, and therefore never
    Shall aught move me from His side;
And to all will I declare,
    That my saving health is He,
And that where He is not, there
    I wish not myself to be.

I believe, and therefore shun not
    Troubles which the Lord ordains;
I believe, and therefore run not,
    But gird up my loins and reins;
Many a victory have I won,
    Oft stood firm by sin enticed;
And by whom was all this done?
    In Thy strength, Lord Jesus Christ.

I believe, and therefore sink not
    Under grief, distress, and pain;
I believe, and therefore shrink not
    E'en from death, for death is gain:
For He gives me health and strength
    Even in the last dread strife,
And shall bring me safe at length
    Into everlasting life.

Suffer not my faith to fail me,
    But uphold me with Thy hand,
That, whatever foes assail me,
    I may reach the promised land.
Jesus, Thou my Joshua be,
    Let me follow in Thy train,
That I may at last with Thee
    In the heavenly Canaan reign.

GOD'S COMMANDMENTS ARE NOT HARD.

T is not after all so hard
   To be a happy man;
We give ourselves unto the Lord,
   And do the best we can.

Not slaves but sons, we gladly do
   Whatever we are told,
And with our love increases too
   Our joy a thousand fold.

We work with silent industry,
   Unconscious of the toil,
As of itself some goodly tree
   Bears fruit in fertile soil.

Our daily task we enter on
   With willing hearts and hands;
The Lord in us hath always done
   What He from us demands.

In all He wills we acquiesce,
   Assured that it is best,
At every time, in every place,
   With Him we must be blest.

Thus doth the Chriſtian thrive and grow,
   Though poor, a wealthy man,
And if we can't be happy ſo,
   I know not how we can.

I WILL ABIDE WITH THEE.

IN Thy service will I ever,
    Jesus, my Redeemer, stay;
Nothing me from Thee shall sever,
    Gladly would I go Thy way.
Life in me Thy life produces,
    And gives vigour to my heart,
As the vine doth living juices
    To the purple grape impart.

Could I be in other places
    Half so happy as with Thee,
Who so many gifts and graces
    Hast Thyself prepared for me?
No place could be half so fitted
    To impart true joy, I ween,
Since to Thee, O Lord, committed
    Power in heaven and earth hath been.

Where shall I find such a Master,
    Who hath done my soul such good,
And retrieved the great disaster
    Sin first caused, by His own blood?
Is not He my rightful owner,
    Who for me His own life gave?
Were it not a foul dishonour
    Not to love Him to the grave?

Yes, Lord Jeſus, I am ever
  Thine in ſorrow and in joy;
Death the union ſhall not ſever,
  Nor Eternity deſtroy.
I am waiting, yea, am ſighing
  For my ſummons to depart;
He is beſt prepared for dying
  Who in life is Thine in heart.

Let Thy light on me be ſhining
  When the day is almoſt gone,
When the evening is declining,
  And the night is drawing on :
Bleſs me, O my Father, laying
  Both Thy hands on my meek head,
" Here thy day is ended," ſaying,
  " Yonder live the faithful dead."

Stay beſide me, when the ſtillneſs
  And the icy touch of death
Fills my trembling ſoul with chillneſs,
  Like the morning's froſty breath;
As my failing eyes grow dimmer,
  Let my ſpirit grow more bright,
As I ſee the firſt faint glimmer
  Of the everlaſting light.

YE SHALL REJOICE WITH UNSPEAKABLE JOY.

HOW shall I describe the pleasure,
   Which penetrates my inmost frame,
That I may call the Lord my treasure,
   My Saviour and Redeemer name;
That in my greatest tribulation
I may find Him my consolation,
And hope, through faith in God's dear Son,
That my true joy has now begun!

Could'st thou once know, O unbeliever,
   The truth to which thou hast been blind,
Thou would'st awake, as from a fever,
   In grief and agony of mind.
Couldst thou but taste one hour the blessing
Of inward peace and joy possessing,
Thou would'st not lose another day,
But come to Christ without delay.

Time was, when I myself have tasted
   The joys this cold world can bestow;
When precious hours in vain I wasted,
   And pierced myself with many a woe;

From flower to flower like insects hasting,
And pleasure after pleasure tasting,
Till pleasure ended, as it must,
In disappointment and disgust.

There cleaves to this world's fleeting pleasures
    The curse of insufficiency,
She spends, but doth not gather treasures
    To last throughout eternity;
Her glittering hoards of boasted treasure
Cannot repair, in smallest measure,
Sin's deadly mischief, or contrive
To save one human soul alive.

How different are the joys which greet us,
    When Jesus hath new life bestowed,
When Peace and Comfort come to meet us
    And scatter flowers upon our road;
When at each hour we find sweet healing
For every wound that we are feeling,
A balsam for our keenest smart,
A welcome to a Father's heart!

Our wants and wishes now are fewer,
    The world around us seems more small;
Our joys are simpler far and truer,
    Unmixed with bitterness and gall.
Modest and humble in successes,
Patient in troubles and distresses,
We are, and 'tis our pride to be,
Our Saviour's rightful property.

Above us lies an open heaven,
　　Beneath us closed a dread abyss;
We love, because we are forgiven,
　　We have true joy, true rest and peace,
Answer to prayer, support in trial,
Some better thing for each denial;
The good thing we have chosen is
Our soul's eternal happiness.

Thus ever happy in possessing
　　The love and favour of our God,
And trusting Him for every blessing
　　Both for our soul's and body's good,
We live prepared always for dying,
Ready to quit this world of sighing,
To reap an undeserved reward,
And be for ever with the Lord.

HEAVENLY GUIDANCE.

PRAISE, all praise, to Thee be given,
    God the Father and the Son!
On the earth and in the heaven
    All has prospered Thou hast done.
I confess with grateful feelings,
Wise and good have been thy dealings;
They proclaim aloud, that he
Is most blest who trusts in Thee.

Blessed Lord, if Thou hadst led me
    As I foolishly desired,
All the good I shunned forbid me,
    Given all that I required;
Hadst Thou punished me by granting
All that I believed was wanting,
Words would not, O God, express
What had been my wretchedness!

How can they, whose eyes are blinded
    'Mid the din and dust of earth,
Find the pearl the heavenly-minded
    Deem of such transcendent worth?
Evil ways perversely choosing,
And the right and true refusing,
Farther every day they stray
From the true and living way.

He who wishes no conductor
   But the hand of his dear Lord,
He who wishes no instructor
   But His Spirit and His word,
He shall walk secure from dangers
In a land of foes and strangers,
Till at last the same wise hand
Brings him to his Fatherland.

Therefore with my God hereafter
   I will patiently abide,
And in spite of sneers and laughter
   Make Him my support and guide.
Since in God I have confided,
I have been securely guided;
What I have experienced, is
My best pledge for future bliss.

God hath said it, God hath said it,
   God hath said, and I obey;
God hath said it, God hath said it,
   And with joy I go my way:
God so willeth, God so willeth,
Every murmur sweetly stilleth,
God so wills it, e'en hath power
To make sweet the last dread hour.

LIFE AND CONTENTMENT IN JESUS.

O BLESSED Sun, whoſe ſplendour
    Diſpels the ſhades of night,
O Jeſus, my defender,
    My ſoul's ſupreme delight,
All day I hear reſounding
    A voice with ſilver tone,
Which ſpeaks of grace abounding
    Through God's eternal Son.

A deep and heavenly feeling
    Oft ſeizes on my breaſt,
Ah! here is balm for healing,
    Here only is true reſt!
Though fortune ſhould bereave me
    Of all I love the beſt,
If Chriſt His love ſtill leave me,
    I freely give the reſt.

To win this precious treaſure
    And matchleſs pearl, I would
Give honour, wealth, and pleaſure,
    And every earthly good;
I gladly would surrender
    The deareſt thing which might
Obſcure my Sun's bright ſplendour,
    And rob me of His light.

I know no life divided,
  O Lord of life, from Thee,
In Thee is life provided
  For all mankind and me:
I know no death, O Jefus,
  Becaufe I live in Thee,
Thy death it is which frees us
  From death eternally.

I fear no tribulation,
  Since, whatfoe'er it be,
It makes no feparation
  Between my Lord and me.
If Thou, my God and teacher,
  Vouchfafe to be my own,
Though poor, I fhall be richer
  Than monarch on his throne.

If, while on earth I wander,
  My heart is light and bleft,
Ah! what fhall I be yonder
  In perfect peace and reft?
O bleffed thought in dying!
  We go to meet the Lord,
Where there fhall be no fighing,
  A kingdom our reward.

Lord, with this truth imprefs me,
  And write it on my heart,
To comfort, cheer, and blefs me,
  That Thou my Saviour art:

Without Thy love to guide me,
  I should be wholly lost,
The floods would quickly hide me
  On life's wide ocean tost.

Thy love it was which sought me,
  Thyself unsought by me,
And to the haven brought me
  Where I would gladly be :
The things, which once distrest me,
  My heart no longer move,
Since this sweet truth imprest me,
  That I possess Thy love.

TURN AGAIN.

URN, poor wanderer, ere the sen-
tence
   Falls on thee which none can stay;
Flee to Christ with deep repentance,
   Seek the Lord without delay.
As thou art, with all thy burden,
Come, and He will grant thee pardon:
See! He comes to meet thee, sealing
   With His own most holy word,
Pardon, blessing, strength, and healing;
   Turn, O turn thee to the Lord.

Flee from worldly dissipation,
   Commune with thy heart, be still;
God shall by thy renovation
   All thy best desires fulfil.
There a peaceful calm awaits thee
From the storm which agitates thee,
There shalt thou discern the warning
   Of the Spirit in thy breast,
Pleading with thee, night and morning,
   Till He brings thee to thy rest.

Lay aside all needless terrors,
   For thy Father's loving heart

Offers pardon for thy errors,
　Balsam for thy keenest smart.
Look on Him, whom thou hast wounded,
Yet whose love hath so abounded,
That He suffered to redeem thee;
　Turn, O turn again, nor fear,
That thy Lord will yet condemn thee,
　Who esteemed thy soul so dear.

Drink in life with deep thanksgiving,
　Dwelling on this gracious theme,
God is patient and forgiving,
　And almighty to redeem;
Not a grief, but He can feel it,
Not a wound, but He can heal it;
He hath balm for every sorrow,
　Cleansing for the vilest sin;
O delay not till to-morrow
　What thou canst this day begin.

Shake off all thy sloth and dulness,
　Linger not, nor take thine ease;
Come from emptiness to fulness,
　Shadows to realities,
Out of dimness into clearness,
Out of distance into nearness!
Come away from sin and sorrow,
　Come to Christ without delay!
Put not off until to-morrow
　What thy God will give to-day.

THE VANITY OF THE WORLD.

CAN then the world make no provision
    For human happiness below?
Is all she gives us but a vision,
    A fleeting dream, an empty show?
Her burthens are so hard to bear,
Her pleasures lighter than the air!

Her life is but a fruitless striving,
    A never fought-out battle-field,
A fruitless toil, a vain contriving,
    A sorrow which remains unhealed,
A sleep which gives no rest, a breath,
An every day repeated death.

Sometimes we spend the hours in trying
    Their weary dulness to beguile,
Now we complain that they are flying,
    And cry, "sweet hours, O stay awhile."
Sometimes we wish to flee away,
Sometimes on earth would ever stay.

Now draughts of flattery we are drinking
    From poisoned cups, and now we try
To drown remorse, and silence thinking,
    By noisy mirth and revelry;

Now scoff at God, and now give vent
To murmuring and discontent.

Meantime both head and heart are hollow
   In midst of riot and excess,
And on enjoyment quickly follow
   Satiety and weariness:
We feast, and yet have not our fill,
We sleep, and yet are weary still.

We make provision every minute
   For the poor tenement of clay,
And leave the soul who dwells within it
   To pine and languish day by day;
The pampered body takes its ease,
She sits at home and languishes.

While thus, uncared for and neglected,
   Averse from God she pines away,
Death comes upon us unexpected,
   And pulling down our house of clay,
Turns out the soul from time, to be
A tenant of eternity.

Make me, O God, not earthly-minded,
   But Thine in Jesus Christ to be,
That by the world no longer blinded,
   I may devote my heart to Thee,
And *in* not *of* the world be found,
A shining light to all around.

OUR CONVERSATION IS IN HEAVEN.

AS a traveller, returning
    To his home from some far land,
Thinks of it with bosom yearning,
    Ere his foot hath touched the
        strand;
So amid the noisy pleasures
    Of the world, the heart oft sighs
For the nobler higher treasures
    Laid up for us in the skies.

All our wish and our endeavour
    Is to love and please and choose
Him, who loves us, nor will ever
    What is for our good refuse.
When the soul without distraction
    Sits and listens at His feet,
Then she finds true satisfaction
    And a happiness complete.

Jesus, like the magnet, raises
    Our dull spirits to the skies,
And we seem, in prayer and praises,
    As on eagles' wings to rise;
Why we feel this strong attraction,
    Why we wait for His command
In each thought, and word, and action,
    Can the world not understand.

Should our enemies asperse us,
 Our dear Lord, who loves us so,
Bids us bless e'en them who curse us,
 And to love our greatest foe.
He, who died for our salvation
 And on us hath heaven bestowed,
Wills that by our conversation
 We should glorify our God.

Can we have our hearts in heaven,
 And yet earthly-minded live?
Can we, who have been forgiven,
 Not forget and not forgive?
Can we hate an erring brother,
 Only love when we are loved,
And not bear with one another,
 By Christ's Holy Spirit moved?

Ah! no hater, or blasphemer,
 None who slander and defame,
Can be one with the Redeemer,
 Who was gentle as a lamb:
Love will cause assimilation
 With the object of our love,
Love will work a transformation
 And renewal from above.

None, O Lord, who are unholy,
 Shall Thy perfect beauty see;
Teach me to be meek and lowly,
 Teach me to resemble Thee.

Keep me from the world unspotted,
   That I may not only be
To Thy service here devoted,
   But abide in heaven with Thee.

THE SERVANT OF THE LORD.

THE man is highly blessed,
    Who makes it his delight,
To do his Master's bidding,
    And serve him day and night;
Who asks him for His blessing,
    When he begins the day,
His sins with grief confessing,
    When he has gone astray.

His loving heart constrains him
    To watch the beckoning hand
Of Him, whose absence pains him,
    Whose wish is a command;
He needs no admonition,
    But follows glad and still,
For love by intuition
    Prevents the loved one's will.

God sanctifies and blesses
    The trials which He sends;
The burthen lightly presses,
    It breaks not, though it bends:
And though our tears flow faster
    At each increasing stroke,
We lean upon our Master,
    And meekly bear His yoke.

We know He sympathises
　　In all that grieves us so,
And no distress despises
　　Which we can undergo:
To Him we may each weakness,
　　Each trouble boldly show,
Who hath for us with meekness
　　Endured such bitter woe.

And when our prospect brightens,
　　And we are light and gay,
He is the sun which lightens,
　　And turns our night to day.
From Him comes every blessing,
　　To Him they lead us back;
In Him all things possessing,
　　No real good we lack.

How sweet a lot befalls us,
　　How greatly are we blest!
For that whereto He calls us,
　　We know is always best:
In good and adverse seasons,
　　In pleasure and in pain,
We ask Him for no reasons,
　　Nor ever once complain.

Brief as a night of slumber
　　Our days glide swiftly on,
Ere we can tell their number
　　Death comes, and we are gone!

O happy day which sees us
    To our Beloved restored!
When we shall be with Jesus,
    The servant with his Lord.

STRONG IN FAITH, RICH IN LOVE.

ET me build on this secure foundation,
　　Lord, my rock, my safety, and my
　　　shield,
　Which Thy holy word for my salva-
　　　tion
Hath in this accepted time revealed :
Jesus Christ His glory hath forsaken,
And our flesh and human nature taken,
　To redeem us by His death from death;
He hath died, that we might be forgiven,
He hath died, that we may live in heaven,
　There by sight, and here meantime by faith.

Plant in me a faith secure and stable
　In the work which Thou, O God, hast planned,
That no sneers nor my own doubts be able
　To destroy the faith wherein I stand.
Give me Peter's sorrow and contrition,
Let me witness also his confession,
　"Thou art Christ, to whom then shall I go?"
Like St. Paul's, let this be my endeavour,
That the life I live I may live ever
　Through the faith of Him who loved me so.

Kindle by the Spirit's inspiration
　That undying love within my heart,

Who, though crowned herself with Thy salvation,
    Yet prefers a servant's humble part,
Who is meek and gentle in behaviour,
Rich in faith, rejoicing in her Saviour,
    Calm and patient under every ill;
Suffers, hopes, believes all things, and blesses
God alike in joy and in distresses,
    Ready both to bear and do His will.

And so let me, loving and confiding,
    Walk conducted by Thy faithful hand,
Or beneath Thy sheltering wings abiding
    Shun the foes which I can not withstand:
Nor, when conquering, let me boast, but rather
Clinging like a child unto its father,
    Smile securely in Thy firm embrace:
Let me on Thy faithful word relying
Clasp Thee with the arms of faith, till dying
    I at length behold Thee face to face.

SALVATION IS COME TO THIS HOUSE.

 HAPPY houſe, O home ſupremely
          bleſt,
      Where Thou, Lord Jeſus Chriſt, art
          entertained
   As the moſt welcome and belovèd
      gueſt,
With true devotion and with love unfeigned :
Where all hearts beat in uniſon with Thine,
   Where eyes grow brighter as they look on Thee,
Where all are ready, at the ſlighteſt ſign,
   To do Thy will and do it heartily.

O happy houſe, where man and wife are one
   Through love of Thee, in ſpirit, heart, and mind;
Together joined by holy bands, which none,
   Not death itſelf, can ſever or unbind :
Where both on Thee unfailingly depend,
   In weal and woe, in good and evil days,
And hope with Thee eternity to ſpend
   In ſweet communion and eternal praiſe.

O happy houſe, where with the hands of prayer
   Parents commit their children to the Friend,
Who, with a more than mother's tender care,
   Will watch and keep them ſafely to the end :

Where they are taught to sit at Jesus' feet,
   And listen to the words of life and truth,
And learn to lisp His praise in accents sweet
   From early childhood to advancing youth.

O happy house, where man and maid pursue
   Their daily labours as unto the Lord,
Desiring only that whate'er they do
   May be according to His will and word:
As servants, yet as friends and brethren too,
   Their love with deep humility combined,
No less in little than in great things true,
   They serve Him gladly with a willing mind.

O happy house, where Thou dost share the weal,
   Where none forget Thee, whatsoe'er befall;
O happy house, where Thou the wounds dost heal,
   The Healer and the Comforter of all;
Till every one his stated task hath done,
   And all at length shall peacefully depart
To the bright realms where Thou Thyself art gone,
   The Father's house where Thou already art.

THE WORD OF LIFE.

WORD of Life, eternal fountain,
    Thou doſt living ſtrength impart
To the ſoul that truly ſeeks Thee,
    To the faint and longing heart:
So ſome tender flower of ſummer
    Drooping in the noonday ſun,
Bends its head, to drink the waters
    Which beſide it ſoftly run.

What were earth, if Thou wert abſent,
    But a vale by ſtreams unfed?
What were heaven without Thy preſence,
    But a hall untenanted?
What were life, by Thee ungladdened,
    But a long protracted death?
What, without Thee, would be dying?
    Night without the morning's breath.

Word of Life, 'tis Thine to light us,
    But 'tis Thine to warn us too;
Thou a glorious heaven revealeſt,
    But bring'ſt alſo hell to view:
Terribly Thou wakeſt ſinners
    From their dull lethargic reſt,
Yet Thy mercy ſweetly covers
    Sins repented and confeſt.

Taught by Thee, we learn to tremble
   At a Judge who all things weighs;
But no lefs to love a Father,
   Who bears with the child that ftrays;
One who gave His own belovèd
   For the fin that He reproves,
Who in Him the fin condemneth,
   Yet in Him the finner loves.

Word of Life, to him that hears thee
   Thou doft promife heavenly reft;
Yet by him alone who keeps thee
   Shall the jewel be poffeft.
Ah, then! I will ever keep thee,
   Word of God, the Spirit's fword;
Help me here to fight and conquer,
   There to reap a bright reward.

THE LIFE OF FAITH.

WHAT greater bleſſedneſs can be,
    What more exalted ſtate,
Than when, O Lord, our lives to Thee
    By faith we conſecrate?

The thought that Thou art ever nigh
    Inſpires us with delight;
We ſeem to ſee Thee with the eye,
    And live as in Thy ſight.

What though our lips oft ſilent be,
    The heart doth always pray,
And grateful thoughts riſe up to Thee,
    O Lord, both night and day.

We may with Thee hold converſe ſweet,
    When all around is ſtill,
And come before Thy mercy-ſeat,
    As often as we will.

Like children at Thy feet we play,
    And ſhould we come to grief,
We fly to Thee to wipe away
    Our tears and grant relief.

When we are weary, our kind God
  Prepares for us a bed,
And covers with the cool green sod
  His sleeping children's head.

There in the deep still night we lie,
  Until the morning break,
And we shall hear the Saviour's cry;
  "Awake from sleep, awake."

What then shall be, to our dim ken
  A mystery doth seem;
We know that we shall be like men
  Awakened from a dream.

UNITY IN THE SPIRIT.

BRETHREN, called by one vocation,
    Members of one family,
Heirs through Chrift of one falvation,
    Let us live in harmony;
  Nor by ftrife
Embitter life,
    Journeying to eternity.

In a land where all are ftrangers,
    And our fojourning fo fhort,
In the midft of common dangers,
    Concord is our beft fupport:
Heart with heart
Divides the fmart,
    Lightens grief of every fort.

Let us fhun all vain contention
    Touching words and outward things,
Whence alas! fo much difsenfion
    And fuch bitter rancour fprings:
Troubles ceafe,
Where Chrift brings peace
    And fweet healing on His wings.

Judge not haftily of others,
    But thine own falvation mind;

Nor be lynx-eyed to thy brother's,
  To thine own offences blind;
God alone
Difcerns thine own,
  And the hearts of all mankind.

Let it be our chief endeavour,
  That we may the Lord obey,
Then fhall envy ceafe for ever,
  And all hate be done away;
Free from ftrife
Shall be his life
  Who ferves God both night and day.

THE BLESSING OF CHRISTIAN FELLOWSHIP.

IT is a practice greatly bleſt
   To ſpeak, Lord Jeſu Chriſt, of Thee;
Thou art amongſt us as a gueſt,
   We feel it, though we cannot ſee:
We ſeem to breathe, in glad ſurpriſe,
   An atmoſphere of love and bliſs,
And read within each other's eyes,
   To whom it is we owe all this.

How quickly ſtrife and envy end,
   How ſoon all idle griefs depart,
When friend takes counſel thus with friend,
   When ſoul meets ſoul, and heart meets heart;
We have ſo many things to ſay,
   So many failings to confeſs,
Time flies alas! ſo ſoon away,
   We cannot half we would expreſs.

How fain would we repeat again
   The touching tale of God's dear Son,
His faithfulneſs and love to men,
   And the great things which He hath done;
How He firſt touched our heart and feelings
   By joy and grief's alternate ſway,
And led us by His gracious dealings
   In ſafety to this very day.

We hear a still small voice within,
    When first He makes His presence known;
Blest hour! when we confess our sin
    With many a self-accusing groan:
When we bow down and humbly call
    On God to heal our bitter smart,
We feel His Spirit gently fall
    Like dew upon our weary heart.

We feel relieved from all distress,
    From anxious doubt and boding fear;
We have a foretaste of our bliss,
    And breathe a purer atmosphere:
We seem new creatures to become,
    New thoughts and hopes possess our mind;
Like wanderers returning home,
    We leave all former things behind.

O let us then, dear Lord, be blest
    With Thy sweet presence every day,
Be with us as our daily guest
    And our companion on the way:
Fan our devotion's feeble flame,
    Let us press on to things before,
Bring us together in Thy name,
    Until we meet to part no more.

COMFORT IN THE NIGHT.

EEP no more, poor child of sorrow,
    O'er thy youth's untimely blight;
Joy will come again to-morrow,
    Grief endureth but a night.

Seems it long till purple morning
    Streaks the eastern sky with light?
Stars with beauty are adorning
    E'en the sable brow of night.

DEVOTION.

OW good it is, Lord, to be here
    Amid the congregation!
The beating heart and gushing tear
    Bespeak our adoration.

Wherefore, ye tear drops, do ye flow?
    O heart, what means this beating?
The body rests from toil below,
    The soul her God is meeting.

WORK IN THE LORD.

WHAT in the Lord thou doeſt muſt
    ſucceed,
  The glory His, the bleſſing ſhall be
    thine ;
From Him alike both will and act
    proceed,
He ſows and gives the increaſe to the ſeed,
  He prompts and perfects every good deſign :
Hands on thy work, thy heart on God alone,
Thus and thus only is a good work done.

Think not that ought is in God's eyes ſo ſmall,
  That He will not the needful ſuccour lend ;
His ear is ever open to thy call,
To give thee ſtrength, to bleſs and proſper all,
  And bring thy labours to a happy end ;
Call on the Lord whate'er thou doſt to bleſs,
And He will crown thy efforts with ſucceſs.

He makes thy heart courageous, firm, and bold,
  And ſhould thy labours ſeem to preſs too ſore,
He ſuffers not thy courage to grow cold,
Smooths on thy care-worn brow the gathering fold,
  Arms thee with patient induſtry, nay more !
Regards the ſmalleſt kindneſs ſhown to one
Of His diſciples, as to Him t'were done.

His presence doth not weaken and destroy,
    But rather strengthens and collects thy powers,
Sheds a bright lustre o'er the day's employ,
Turns toil to pleasure, trouble into joy,
    And gilds with sunshine e'en thy darkest hours:
For what thy hand hath done with all its might,
The Lord will richly to thy heart requite.

How blest to have the Lord before our eyes!
    To speak with Him, and listen to His voice,
With Him in all our troubles to advise,
To feed upon His holy mysteries,
    And in each act of goodness to rejoice;
The world astonished cannot understand
The cheerful promptness of thy heart and hand.

THE MISSIONARIES.

BLEST are ye, ye chosen bearers
    Of God's word to lands afar,
Bidding all men to be sharers
    Of the joyful news ye bear.
Onward, onward, boldly pressing
    Through the howling desert speed,
God will crown your work with blessing,
    And give increase to the seed.

High your Saviour's banner waving,
    Tell it forth, intrepid band,
That His name alone is saving,
    That all power is in His hand.
Be to all the world a witness
    Of the everlasting word,
Teaching all to taste its sweetness,
    And confess that He is Lord.

Arm, ye soldiers, though your weapons
    Be not spears or glittering swords,
Press on still, though danger threatens,
    For the whole earth is the Lord's.
He who sent you will defend you,
    And your King and Shepherd be,
Though like sheep 'mid wolves He send you,
    Ye shall wander glad and free.

Love it was for one another
  Which firſt moved and urged you on,
That to do for your poor brother
  Which the Lord for you hath done.
Therefore ſeek ye neither pleaſure,
  Honour, wealth, nor earthly good,
No! ye bear a nobler treaſure,
  Peace through Jeſus' precious blood.

Bear all hardſhips unrepining,
  Scoffed at, anſwer not a word;
For all lands ſhall ſoon be ſhining
  With the glory of the Lord.
Bleſt are ye, brave ſtandard-bearers,
  Witneſſes for Chriſt to men,
Ye ſhall in His joy be ſharers,
  When your Lord ſhall come again.

After all their tribulations,
  Thouſands ſhall Hoſanna ſing,
And the heavens with acclamations
  To their God and Saviour ring.
Thouſands then ſhall hail the teachers,
  Who firſt brought them to the Lord;
Then ſhall be, ye faithful preachers,
  Your bright crown and ſweet reward.

THE FATHER LOVETH YOU.

HOW bleſt are we! that God of us
  Vouchſafes to be ſo heedful,
Providing for our daily uſe
  Whatever things are needful:
  All things are his,
Whoſe Father is
The God, who ever liveth,
And every good gift giveth.

What though we roam the wide world o'er,
  And have no earthly treaſure,
Our Father's love can give us more
  Than worlds of wealth can meaſure:
   We need not fear,
   Though we have here
But little food and raiment,
Nor aught to give in payment.

He who for us ſo much hath done
  To purchaſe our ſalvation,
Who gave His own belovèd Son
  For our propitiation;
  He who beſtows
  Such love on foes,
Will He, our God and Father,
Not care for us much rather?

Before a throne of grace we may
    Prefent ourfelves with boldnefs,
Nor fear that He will turn away
    His face from us with coldnefs:
He will and can
Hear every man,
Who offers his petition
With faith and true contrition.

In Jefus Chrift the Father's heart
    Is open to receive us;
We fly to it, when inward fmart
    And outward troubles grieve us:
There we may reft
Secure and bleft,
Expofed no more to dangers,
To care and forrow ftrangers.

Think ye the near approach of death
    Can make our hearts feel fadly?
Ah, no, when "Come" the Father faith,
    We will go home right gladly:
Far better 'twere
That we were there!
O would that He would call us!
We figh, when griefs befall us.

He loveth us, that is enough
    To fill our hearts with gladnefs,
He loveth us, that is enough
    To chafe away all fadnefs:

Lord, grant that we
May alſo Thee
Love with a love unceaſing,
Yea, every day increaſing!

FAITHFULNESS IN LITTLE THINGS.

THAT love is pureſt and moſt true,
    Which leans upon its Saviour's breaſt,
And thinks with pleaſure ever new
    How in all things to pleaſe Him beſt;
Which in all things, not great alone,
    On ſerving Him is fully bent,
And knowingly will not to one,
    No! not the ſmalleſt ſin conſent.

For know, my ſoul, the Lord will not
    Hold thy leaſt ſervice in contempt,
For little acts are moſt from ſpot
    Of vanity and pride exempt:
Begin then firſt with little things,
    The ſmalleſt ſin avoid and hate;
Obedience to love adds wings,
    And little faith will grow to great.

If thou avoideſt but the great
    And groſſer ſins, from fear of ſhame,
And doſt the ſmall ones tolerate,
    Thy love is but an empty name;

That is not loving Christ alone,
   That is but loving Him in part,
Not doing His will, but thine own,
   Not serving Him with all thy heart.

For he who is indeed the Lord's,
   Follows Him always, and will shun
In all his actions, thoughts, and words,
   All sin, or an approach to one;
Seeks to promote his Saviour's praise
   In everything he doth and saith,
And walks in His most holy ways,
   Partaker of His life and death.

In every work, and at all hours,
   His chief aim is to serve his Lord
With all his heart, and mind, and powers,
   In strict obedience to His word;
For Him he shrinks not night and day
   From hardship, trouble, loss, and woe;
It is enough for him to say;
   "My Lord commands and wills it so."

Wrestle, my soul, and strive and pray,
   Thyself to this true love to raise,
That thus thou mayst from day to day
   Bring forth new fruit to His great praise:
Study to please Him, and be true,
   My soul, in great and small things both,
For earnest diligence may do
   What is impossible to sloth.

Say not, I will in some great trial
  My constancy and truth maintain;
O think of Peter's sad denial,
  And confidence, which proved so vain:
Then learn to practise truth in small
  As well as in great things; lest thou,
Like Peter, should bewail thy fall,
  Thy faithlessness and broken vow.

I AND MY HOUSE WILL SERVE THE LORD.

I AND my houſe are ready, Lord,
With hearts that beat in ſweet accord,
   To ſerve Thee and obey Thee;
Be in the midſt of us, we pray,
To guide and bleſs us, that we may
   A willing ſervice pay Thee:
Of us all,
Great and ſmall,
Make a pious congregation,
Pure in life and converſation.

Let Thy good Spirit by the word
Work mightily in us, O Lord,
   Our ſouls and bodies filling!
O let the Sun of grace ſhine bright,
That there may be abundant light
   In us and in our dwelling:
On our way,
Night and day,
With the heavenly manna feed us,
To the heavenly Canaan lead us.

Send peace and bleſſing from above,
Unite us all in faith and love
   Who in this houſe are living;

Let charity our hearts prepare
To suffer long and all things bear,
   Meek, gentle, and forgiving:
Nor in aught
Christ hath taught
Let us fail to one another,
But each love and help his brother.

Lord, let our house be built upon
Thy faithfulness and grace alone;
   And when the day is closing,
And night her gloomy shadow flings,
Let us lie down beneath Thy wings
   With childlike trust reposing;
E'en with smart
In the heart,
Cheerful, happy, and confiding,
Patiently in Thee abiding.

If Thou shouldst bless our home with wealth,
Let not the world creep in by stealth,
   And take away the blessing;
For if our hearts should empty be
Of meekness and humility,
Although all else possessing,
We should miss
That true bliss,
Which not all the world's vast treasure
Can supply in smallest measure.

But this, O Lord, we pray for most,
That in our house the Holy Ghost

    May ever be prefiding ;
He can preferve our fouls from fin,
Keep order and found difcipline,
    His Spirit all things guiding :
O may we
Ever be
By the Spirit thus attended
Till our pilgrimage is ended !

THE HAPPY LOT.

UR lot is fall'n in pleasant places,
   A goodly heritage is ours;
To Him, whence come all gifts and graces,
   Let us give praise with all our powers;
He chooses us of His free grace,
And makes us His peculiar race.

He undertook our souls' salvation,
   Our sad condition moved Him so,
And came to us, from pure compassion,
   To raise us from our depths of woe;
O wonderful surpassing love,
Which brought Him to us from above!

He saw in us no real beauty,
   No virtue, nor intrinsic worth;
Not one there was that did his duty,
   For all were sinners from their birth;
Nor was there one, in such distress,
Who could our misery redress.

Then, moved at heart with deep compassion,
   The Lord stretched out His arm to save,

And His own life for our salvation
   And therewith all things freely gave,
Adoption, sonship, and with this
A whole eternity of bliss.

O Lord, of goodness so amazing
   Not one is worthy, no! not one;
We stand in shame and wonder gazing
   At the great things which Thou hast done;
Thy crowning grace and precious blood
Have reconciled us with our God.

We feel quite certain of obtaining
   Nothing but goodness from Thy hand,
And wend our way without complaining
   Through dreary mist and barren land,
With heaven in view, where we shall be
Joined thro' eternity to Thee.

The lines are fall'n in pleasant places,
   A goodly heritage is ours,
And gladly would we share the graces
   Which God's great goodness richly showers;
We offer them alike to all
Who will obey the gracious call.

It grieves us sore when men refuse them,
   And treat our offers with disdain,
Or by neglect for ever lose them,
   And make the grace of God in vain;
All ye who thirst, come here and buy,
And Christ will all your wants supply.

ABIDE IN JESUS.

O ABIDE, abide in Jesus,
   Who for us bare griefs untold,
And Himself, from pain to ease us,
   Suffered pangs a thousandfold:
Bide with Him, who still abideth
   When all else shall pass away,
And as Judge supreme presideth
   In that dread and awful day.

All is dying: hearts are breaking,
   Which to ours were once fast bound,
And the lips have ceased from speaking,
   Which once uttered such sweet sound,
And the arms are powerless lying,
   Which were our support and stay,
And the eyes are dim and dying,
   Which once watched us night and day.

Everything we love and cherish
   Hastens onward to the grave,
Earthly joys and pleasures perish,
   And whate'er the world e'er gave;
All is fading, all is fleeing,
   Earthly flames must cease to glow,
Earthly beings cease from being,
   Earthly blossoms cease to blow.

Yet unchanged, while all decayeth,
   Jefus ftands upon the duft;
" Lean on me alone," He fayeth,
   " Hope and love and firmly truft!"
O abide, abide with Jefus,
   Who Himfelf for ever lives,
Who from death eternal frees us,
   Yea, who life eternal gives.

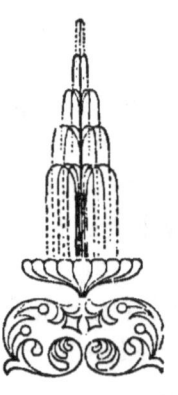

THE CHRISTIAN'S CROSS.

THE badge the Christian wears on earth,
   Is his dear Saviour's cross,
And he who understands its worth,
   Regards all else as dross.

He wears it humbly, not for show,
   But as a cure for sin;
Not shining on his breast, ah no!
   He wears his cross within.

And tho' it tries and grieves him too,
   He is no less content;
He knows both what 'tis meant to do,
   And by whom it is sent.

He wears it for a brief space here,
   But as a pledge in hand
Of the bright crown, which he shall wear
   In his dear Fatherland.

BE READY, FOR THE DAYS ARE EVIL.

ET me suffer wrong without complaining,
　While myself from doing wrong abstaining,
　　Through Thy grace and strength,
　　　O Lord, I pray!
Let me never smite the hand that smites me,
But do good to him who ill requites me;
　Thus prepare me for the evil day.

Into Thine own image, Lord, transform me,
To Thy gentle Spirit so conform me,
　That this lesson never may be lost,
Not the poor oppressed, but the oppressor,
Not the injured, but the proud transgressor,
　Is the man who needs our pity most.

Though by cruel treatment oft incited,
Thou hast never ill with ill requited,
　Nor reviled hast Thou reviled again;
Yet it must have grieved Thy holy nature,
More, far more than me a sinful creature,
　To behold the wickedness of men.

Thou hadſt power not only to create us,
But to puniſh and annihilate us;
  Yet ſo great, ſo wonderful Thy love!
That to ſave us from the doom impending,
Thou didſt give Thyſelf to death, deſcending
  To our depth from Thy great height above.

My true Peace and Saviour, be Thou near me,
That in ſuffering I may not grow weary;
  Be Thou near me to direct my way;
Strengthen Thou my ſoul when foes aſſail her,
That Thy patient Spirit may not fail her;
  Thus prepare me for the evil day.

That herſelf in patience ſtill poſſeſſing,
She may find e'en woes to be a bleſſing,
  Nor account them ſtrange when they ariſe;
Point her to the happy realms above her,
Where departed ſaints, who dearly love her,
  Wait to greet her in the opening ſkies.

LONGING.

 THAT my soul might never lack
    The guidance of Thy gentle hand,
But follow in the easy track
    Of Thy sweet will and wise com-
        mand!
That I might find the Lord's employ
Not a hard service but a joy!

O that each word of Thine I thought
    Deserving of my high esteem,
And all opposed to it as naught
    But falsehood and an idle dream!
That my sole aim in all might be,
To do, dear Lord, what pleases Thee!

O that I made Thy word a light,
    My standard and my last appeal,
To shew me what is wrong or right,
    What hurtful, what for my true weal,
Not ever doubtful what I would
When I know plainly what I should.

O that to every word I paid
    A due observance and regard,
Nor sought Thy precepts to evade
    When clear, because they seem too hard,

And that, albeit weak and faint,
I followed them without complaint!

Then life were one confiftent whole,
   Not a mixed web of ill and good,
The full furrender of the foul,
   A victory over flefh and blood;
Then fhould I find, made glad and free,
Thy fervice perfect liberty.

O make Thy precepts fweet to me
   By Thy good Spirit's gentle fway,
And let my feet be led by Thee
   In Thine own true and perfect way;
Thy precepts are my life's true blifs,
At once its rule and happinefs.

With all Thy law's exact demands
   O make me by Thy grace content,
That I may do what it commands,
   Not from the fear of punifhment,
No! but becaufe my heart relies
Upon Thy grace and facrifice.

MY SOUL THIRSTETH AFTER THE LIVING GOD.

ASK not, what it is that ails me,
    Probe not deep my inward smart;
God it is Himself that fails me,
    Thirst for God consumes my heart;
For alas! if He be wanting,
    Boundless wealth would leave me poor,
Houseless, friendless, thirsty, fainting,
    Wandering from door to door.

Riches, honour, pomp, and learning,
    Beauty, pleasure, science, art,
Cannot satisfy my yearning,
    Cannot fill my aching heart;
Patience under tribulation,
    Strength to suffer, love, and live,
Joy in death and consolation,
    God Himself alone can give.

Idols of the heathen nations,
    Works of art and human skill,
Cannot quench my aspirations,
    Nor my earnest longings still;
Subtle thoughts and speculations
    Of past ages and our own
Cannot reach my expectations,
    Which cry out for God alone.

When shall I appear before Thee,
   When behold Thy glorious face,
And with joyful lips adore Thee,
   In Thy full unclouded grace?
When shall love succeed to coldness,
   Confidence to doubt and fear,
When shall I with childlike boldness
   To the throne of grace draw near?

When will God be my sole treasure,
   When will He abide with me?
When will His great will the measure
   Of my will and actions be?
When will no thought ever enter
   Into heart and mind but this,
In the Lord alone to centre
   Every hope of happiness?

No! the flame, which He hath lighted,
   Will not prove a flickering ray,
He who hath this thirst excited,
   Will its longing quench one day;
When I quit this vale of sadness,
   And to brighter regions soar,
I shall drink with joy and gladness
   Living waters evermore.

ENCOURAGEMENT.

LONG and toilsome is the road,
    Difficult the track,
And beneath its heavy load
    Often bows our back,
Yet our hearts feel no dismay;
Though our strength be small,
On His strength we well may stay,
    Who is Lord of all.

Jesus never will forget us;
    On His word we stay,
That He will not leave, nor let us
    Perish on the way:
Often when our strength appears
    To forsake us quite,
Comfort whispers in our ears;
    "He will set all right."

He who brought the crystal wave
    From its rocky bed,
And the Prophet in the cave
    By the ravens fed;
He who with a little bread
    Thousands satisfied,
Can He not for those who need
    Even now provide?

He who in His hands doth bear
    This terrestrial ball,
And without whom not a hair
    From our head doth fall;
Who the great thinks not too great,
    Nor the small too small,
Can He see our sad estate,
    Heedless of our call?

He who opened heaven to man,
    And hath plainly shewed
By what way we may and can
    Reach that blest abode;
He who to prepare a place
    Hath such pains bestowed,
Can He let His chosen race
    Perish on the road?

No! He neither can nor will;
    God is very good,
And the promise will fulfil
    Sealed by His own blood.
Courage then, tho' hard your lot,
    God can never lie,
Lift your heads on high, fear not,
    Your redemption's nigh.

THE PLANT OF GOD'S PLANTING.

EXCITE in me, O Lord, an ardent thirst
   After Thy kingdom and its righteousness,
And smite my stony heart, that tears may burst
Of true repentance and of deep distress.
Alas! the garden of my heart is cumbered
With hidden tares and noxious weeds unnumbered;
O cleanse Thou me, that I may all my days
Bring forth good fruit to Thy eternal praise!

I know that from Thy fostering care proceed,
   Thou heavenly gardener, sower of the earth,
The sprouting, growth, and ripening of the seed,
   Through all its stages from its earliest birth:
There's not a flower so mean, nor blade that groweth,
Whereon Thy love no tender care bestoweth;
How sweet to think, Lord, that on Thee depend
Germ, blossom, fruit, until my life shall end!

Thy hand first drew me from the earth's green lap,
   With light revived me, and with soft dew fed,
And when a storm befell me, the mishap
   Turned to my good, and raised my drooping head.

From day to day Thy goodnefs more amazes,
And fills my heart with gratitude and praifes;
And thus I welcome, purging me from fin,
Thy needful pruning and wife difcipline.

A TIME OF DEARTH.

OUR life is often dark,
　　Our foul of joy bereft,
　It feems as though no fpark
　　Of faith or love were left;
　The hope, which once was ours,
　　Has fled we know not why,
And yet thefe very hours
　　Are bleffings from on high.

When God awhile His face
　　Thus hides from us, we learn
To prize the more His grace,
　　And long for its return;
The foul with all her might,
　　Like Jacob, ftrives and pleads,
And wreftles day and night
　　Till fhe at laft fucceeds.

Ah! then we feel full well
　　How fad our life would prove,
More fad than words can tell,
　　Without the Saviour's love;
'Tis that which renders fweet
　　The cup of bitternefs,
And foothes the grief we meet
　　In this world's wildernefs.

These are the soul's true fast,
  When all is dark within,
And we can only taste
  The bitterness of sin;
Yet all is kindly meant,
  And by this very fast,
More truly we repent,
  And feast with joy at last.

The Lord knows when to bless,
  As well as to correct,
And oft relieves distress,
  When we the least expect;
Yea! often doth He make
  The cloud we so much dread
In showers refreshing break
  Upon our weary head.

In times like these we should
  Be driven to despair,
And in desponding mood
  Give up all hope and prayer,
Did God before our eyes
  Not set forth His dear Son,
His death and sacrifice,
  And all that He has done.

Then learn to comprehend
  The dealings of thy God,
To mark their gracious end,
  And meekly kiss the rod;

With patience wait awhile
  The issue of thy woes,
Soon shall the desert smile,
  And blossom like the rose.

FATHER, SON, AND HOLY GHOST.

Father, whose hand hath led me so
    securely,
Father, whose ear hath listened to
    my prayer,
Father, whose eye hath watched o'er
    me so surely,
Whose heart hath loved me with a love so rare;
Vouchsafe, O heavenly Father, to instruct me
    In the straight way wherein I ought to go,
To life eternal and to heaven conduct me,
    Through health and sickness, and through weal
    and woe.

O my Redeemer, who hast my redemption
    Purchased and paid for by Thy precious blood,
Thereby procuring an entire exemption
    From the dread wrath and punishment of God;
Thou who hast saved my soul from condemnation,
    Redeem it also from the power of sin,
Be thou the Captain still of my salvation,
    Through whom alone I can the victory win.

O Holy Ghost, who from the Father flowest
    And from the Son, O teach me how to pray;
Thou, who the love and peace of God bestowest,
    With faith and hope inspire and cheer my way;

Direct, control, and sanctify each motion
    Within my soul, and make it thus to be
Prayerful, and still, and full of deep devotion,
    A holy temple worthy, Lord, of Thee.

COMFORT.

HOW many hours of gladneſs
    Hath the Lord on us beſtowed,
And how oft in times of ſadneſs
    Eaſed our boſom of its load!

O how oft hath He relieved us
    By the noon-day heat oppreſt,
And how oft, when aught hath grieved us,
    Have we found with Him ſweet reſt!

Short the ſpace, and He will take us
    To Himſelf—O wondrous love!
And of His great glory make us
    Sharers in the realms above.

Then ſhall we appear before Him
    Not as now in pilgrim-dreſs,
But to worſhip and adore Him
    Clothed in robes of righteouſneſs.

Should not that, my heart, compoſe thee
    Under every kind of ill?
Should it not at once diſpoſe thee
    Both to do and bear His will?

All has furthered thy falvation,
   Since thou madeſt Chriſt thy friend;
Wait with peaceful expectation,
   Patiently await the end.

Even things which moſt diſtreſs thee,
   That which moſt thy patience tries,
Are intended all to bleſs thee,
   Are but mercies in diſguiſe.

If He lets thee ſometimes ſtumble
   On the ſteep and rugged way,
'Tis to make thee meek and humble,
   And on Him more fully ſtay.

Onward preſs with look directed
   To thy home beyond the ſkies,
Till the glory long expected
   Burſt on thee in Paradiſe.

Let not threats or hardſhips move thee,
   Soon thy warfare will be done;
Hark! the blue expanſe above thee
   Seems to whiſper " haſten on."

PILGRIM'S SONG.

UNCOMPLAINING, though with care grown hoary,
I defire to wear no crown of glory,
   Where my Saviour wore a crown of thorn;
Not in paths of rofes would I dally,
Where my Saviour trod the gloomy valley,
   Where He fuffered bitter pain and fcorn.

Lord, fend forth Thy light and truth to lead me
In the way, wherein Thy faints precede me,
   With the Holy Spirit for my guide;
Let me choofe the path of felf-denial,
Shunning no fharp crofs or bitter trial
   Which my Saviour's fteps have fanctified.

Give me, Thou, who art the foul's renewer,
Steadfaft faith, which day by day grows truer;
   Kindle love, the fruit of faith, in me,
Love, which puts the foul in active motion,
Love, which fills the heart with true devotion,
   And which leads me thro' the world to Thee.

Many a painful ftep muft be afcended,
Ere my weary pilgrimage is ended,
   And in heaven I fee Thee face to face;
O then reach Thy hand, dear Lord, to raife me!
For alas! the giddy height difmays me,
   Guide, uphold me with Thine arm of grace!

On the wide world's ocean rudely driven,
Let me gaze upon Thine own blue heaven,
   The sweet haven where I long to be;
Give me now the comfort of possessing
What I value as the highest blessing,
   Perfect peace through steadfast faith in Thee.

Here I am a sojourner and stranger,
Worn with hardship and exposed to danger,
   Like a pilgrim with my staff in hand;
With the cross upon my breast I wander
To the promised Canaan which lies yonder,
   My beloved and longed-for Fatherland.

PARTING.

How mean ye thus by weeping
    To break my very heart?
We both are in Chrift's keeping,
    And cannot therefore part;
    Nor time, nor place, can fever
The bonds which us have bound;
In Chrift abide for ever
    Who once in Him are found.

As though to part for ever
    We prefs each other's hands,
And yet no power can fever
    Our love's eternal bands;
We look quite broken-hearted,
    And fob our laft farewell,
And yet can not be parted,
    For both in Jefus dwell.

We fay "I here, you yonder,"
    "You go, and I remain,"
And yet are not afunder,
    But links of one great chain;
In tones of deep affection
    "Our road parts here" we fay,
Yet go in one direction,
    And in the felf-fame way.

Then let us cease from weeping,
   And moderate our woe,
We both are in Christ's keeping,
   With whom we always go;
Both under His protection,
   Both led by His dear hand,
Both in the same direction,
   To the same Fatherland.

In fruitless lamentation
   Let us not waste the hours,
But find our consolation
   In knowing Christ is ours;
If faith in Him unite us,
   Though parting gives us pain,
It cannot disunite us,
   For both in Him remain.

HOME-SICKNESS.

H! how empty is the heart
  In the midſt of pleaſure,
And how fain would we depart
  To our heavenly treaſure.

Threadbare now our garb with age
  Still repair is needing,
And our feet with pilgrimage
  Painful are and bleeding.

Gladly would we be at home,
  Free from toil and dangers,
And no longer houſeleſs roam
  In a land of ſtrangers.

Gladly lay aſide the load
  Which our fleſh inherits,
Worſhipping and ſerving God
  With the ranſomed ſpirits.

But ſince Thou doſt yet delay
  To Thyſelf to take us,
Lord, prepare us while we ſtay,
  Meet for heaven make us.

Richly shall we then be blest,
 When, our warfare ending,
We enjoy the promised rest
 With our Lord ascending.

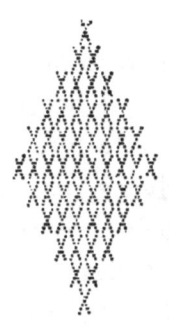

THE SONG OF DYING.

I SING of death and dying,
 A solemn farewell lay,
Which bids thee to be ready
 If death should come this day;
Before the sun declineth
 Thy course may ended be,
And when again it shineth,
 It may not shine on thee.

What is there more uncertain
 Than life, a fleeting breath,
Or what more sure or certain
 Than dying, parting, death?
Our death is drawing nearer
 At every step we take,
Our heart's delights are dying,
 And with them our hearts break.

With staff in hand we journey
 Like pilgrims to the grave,
The monarch's golden sceptre
 Is but a pilgrim's stave.
The earth on all bestoweth
 A garment at our birth,
Upon the earth we wear it,
 And leave it to the earth.

Pafs rugged heights and valleys,
   Climb mountains, if ye will,
Yet can ye not get over
   Yon little grave's green hill;
Thou canft not get beyond it,
   Though it be e'er fo fmall,
For other hands within it
   Will lay both thee and all.

Then fing of death and dying,
   That ancient pilgrim lay,
Becaufe thy feet draw nearer
   Thy grave from day to day;
Let it be wafted o'er thee,
   Like diftant vefper bell,
And not alone of dying,
   But of thy rifing tell.

CHRIST HAS TAKEN AWAY THE POWER OF DEATH.

WHEN comes the hour which seals my doom,
   My heart has ceased from beating,
And laid within the silent tomb
   I wait the final meeting;
How dreadful then would be my fate,
Had Christ not opened heaven's gate
   To every true believer.

How quickly flee our joys away,
   When cruel Death appeareth!
And leave poor feeble man a prey
   To that which most he feareth;
Delusive pleasures quickly flee
Before the stern reality
   Of death, the grave, and judgment.

Guilt now appears without disguise,
   And fills us with confusion,
While falls the bandage from our eyes
   Of pride and self-delusion;
Our stedfast gaze now turned within,
We see our misery and sin
   In all their hateful colours.

Wert Thou not, Lord, in that dread hour
    My joy and confolation;
Didft Thou not bring to me with power
    The tidings of falvation,
That Death has loft his power and fting
For thofe who to Thy crofs do cling,
    My heart would fink within me.

But now fince Thou art mine, I Thine,
    I may have peace in dying,
Thy holy merit 'is made mine,
    From all things juftifying;
Thou haft atonement wrought for me,
And thereby made my death to be
    A reft and peaceful flumber.

Therefore, my Saviour and my God,
    Be Thou in death befide me,
Nor let the comfort of Thy rod
    Be in that hour denied me;
That thus the hour I yield my breath
Be not a ficknefs unto death,
    But unto life eternal.

THE GRAVE.

ESIDE the dark grave ſtanding,
    We ſow in ſilent tears
The ſeed of incorruption,
    The pilgrim full of years.

His home is reached already,
    We ſtill are on the road,
Death was the gate of heaven,
    It took him to his God.

He ſees what we but look for,
    He hath what we ſtill lack,
The foe no more can ſpoil him,
    Who ſtill beſets our track.

His diſembodied ſpirit
    Is with the Lord at reſt,
And while we ſtill are weeping,
    He is ſupremely bleſt.

He wears a crown of glory,
    And lifts the palm on high,
And ſwells with ſaints and angels
    The chorus of the ſky.

We still, poor weary pilgrims,
  In this dark valley roam,
Until again we see him
  And share his happy home.

WHAT WE SHALL BE.

HAT shall we be, and whither shall
  we go,
When the last conflict of our life is
  o'er,
And we return from wandering to
  and fro
  To our dear home through heaven's eternal door!
When we shake off the last dust from our feet,
  When we wipe off the last drop from our brow,
And our departed friends once more shall greet,
  The hope which cheers and comforts us below!

What shall we be, when we ourselves shall see
  Bathed in the flood of everlasting light,
And from all guilt and sin entirely free
  Stand pure and blameless in our Maker's sight;
No longer from His holy presence driven,
  Conscious of guilt, and stung with inward pain,
But friends of God and citizens of heaven,
  To join the ranks of His celestial train!

What shall we be, when we drink in the sound
  Of heavenly music from the spheres above,
When golden harps to listening hosts around
  Declare the wonders of redeeming love;

When far and wide through the resounding air
   Loud Hallelujahs from the ransomed rise,
And holy incense, sweet with praise and prayer,
   Is wafted to the Highest through the skies!

What shall we be, when the freed soul can rise
   With unrestrained and bold aspiring flight
To Him, who by His wondrous sacrifice
   Hath opened heaven, and scattered sin's dark night;
When from the eye of faith the thin veil drops,
   Like wreaths of mist before the morning's rays,
And we behold, the end of all our hopes,
   The Son of God in full refulgent blaze!

What shall we be, when we shall hear Him say;
   "Come, O ye blessed," when we see Him stand,
Robed in the light of everlasting day,
   Before the throne of God at His right hand;
When we behold the eyes from which once flowed
   Tears o'er the sin and misery of man,
And the deep wounds from which the precious blood,
   That made atonement for the world, once ran!

What shall we be, when hand in hand we go
   With blessed spirits risen from the tomb,
Where streams of living water softly flow,
   And trees still flourish in primeval bloom;
Where in perpetual youth no cheek looks old
   By the sharp tooth of cruel time imprest,
Where no bright eye is dimm'd, no heart grows cold,
   No grief, no pain, no death invades the blest!

What shall we be, when every glance we cast
    At the dark valley underneath our feet,
And every retrospect of troubles past
    Makes heaven brighter and its joys more sweet;
When the remembrance of our former woe
    Gives a new relish to our present peace,
And draws our heart to Him, to whom we owe
    Our past deliverance and our present bliss!

What shall we be, who have in Christ believed,
    What through His grace will be our sweet reward!
Eye hath not seen, ear heard, or heart conceived,
    What God for those who love Him hath prepared:
Let us the steep ascent then boldly climb,
    Our toil and labour will be well repaid;
Let us haste onward, till in God's good time
    We reap the fruit, a crown that doth not fade.

FINIS.

www.ingramcontent.com/pod-product-compliance
Lightning Source LLC
Chambersburg PA
CBHW030319170426
43202CB00009B/1063